Janel,

thanks for supporting our
dreams! Come see us live
Hope you enjoy the book

No teeth comes w/o more
Questioning

QUESTION OF . . .

QUESTION OF . . .

SHAWN SIMMONS

To order additional copies of this book, contact:

Xlibris Corporation

1-888-7-XLIBRIS

www.Xlibris.com

Orders@Xlibris.com

CONTENTS

Dedicated to my mother, Nancy Rose
Who has taught me patience, strength and love.
She has been a salvation for me and a saint for all.

CAUTION:

Writings and feelings inside are intense and may not be appropriate for all readers. The closed minded and ignorant need not read. Children, go find a Dr. Seuss book. (I love Dr. Seuss!)
Reader discretion is advised.

FORWARD

We have been cultivated and raised in this societal fallacy. A lie that health is seen in food groups and football games and futile attempts at fortune. Get rich quick, loose weight quicker and sell your soul to save this starving child in some country you should have learned about in fifth grade. Unfortunately we fell asleep in that class. We were dreaming of true communism. Not the garbage of the Curtains of War, because that was a distorted lie as well. I preach the true love of thy neighbor. Raw, true humanity, as we see in abstract conviction, question this dream, more radical I question this paper mache life we erected as the norm . . .

Lost, that's all we are.

. . . Lost sheep, following an ideal fallacy that has been replaced more times than the fashions we adorn our bodies with to hide the fact that we are sheep. We are sheep without wool of our own; synthetic wool, synthetic lies, synthetic motor oil. We have no redeeming value but the ability to question.

But what shall we question?

Is it the question of? I believe so.

What lies in the minds of youth gone astray? What lies in the fingertips of babies whose fingertips take lives? We live in a world where babies breed babies in a stew of spite and hate. When hate is absent, it is replaced by complacency. Complacency breeds into rage, the byproduct of hate. The very breeding of lust in the groins of children yields questions. Vaginal births videotaped steal the momentary perfection of life, love and the pursuit of . . .

What is between her legs?

What question can honestly give us the one true answer of innocence?

What holds the fruit of sanity firmly in its fragile place? What gives man the testicular fortitude to have the courage to walk? Walk alone, walk together, and walk into the sphere of imagination, through integrity captured in moments of loss. Moments of lust, of love, of reverence, irreverence and of what lies beyond the spheres of human comprehension, what does lie beyond? What happens when one goes off the beaten trail?

What are the limits of lost carbon life forms?

What are the questions of . . .?

Unity has become as cliché as simile. Questioning the captivity of the captivated generation of irrevocable comprehension of flower children. The sixties gave us acid, reefer, free sexual experimentation, peace, love and Woodstock. The 70's gave us Kiss. What do we have now in the new millenium? We have contradictions, rebellions and questions. Questions that have answers that we mounted behind pretty venetian blinds. We can twirl a rod and endure the antithesis of everything stood for by whom? By the brick stucco attached to the window, behind the blinds. Look outside and all you see is brick or as I call it, a cliché.

What . . .

Who . . .

Question reality because it has questions for you. Questions that cannot be rationalized by humanistic wisdom, common sense of/from a textbook. No home remedies can give answers to what we lick from the shaft of the lollypop. Smear some butter on the burn, the burn from the sliding of your bareback across the shag rugs. Candy coated questions from the teacher scared to ask herself why she has rugs covering her hardwood floor.

What is she hiding?

What are you hiding?

Question lust in its momentary beastiality, in its sadism, in its beauty. Question that. Coax answers from under the satin sheets tracing the misunderstood edges. You know the edges of the sun and sky or the thrill of X and the bankruptcy of values. Question violence from the standpoint of my face against your baseball bat. The blood, the semen and the mixing of HIV infested fluid as we terminate each other's existence. While we laugh as you make off with five bucks, a shekel and a picture of some woman I lusted for when I was twelve.

Question.

Question your eyes, your understanding and even your existence. This is the Question of . . .

The question of . . .

I know I made you blush. I know your questions have no answers but the hollow caverns of your missing mind. The mind I have numbed with my words and my interrogation. An interrogation that has left many questions still unanswered, and spawned many new questions.

Naked eyes, naked heart, bare shadows baring blush. Welcome to my purity. A purity that knows no question is trivial, and no observation comes without more questioning.

KNOW ME

hello friendly,
    (unfriendly)
      faces of the world
          as a whole,
           in whole.
i'm sorry, i don't know your story.
      (can i tell you mine?)
i want to know your pains,

                  maybe even your joys.
i fancy to feel your anguish,

                  your past.
might you feel the same?
your different!

                  i'm different!
                  we are eclectic!
we feel the same,

                  can we be the same?
what is that in your hand?
why do you want to hurt me?

attack me with your words.
attack me with your fists
just let me know you fucking recognize me.
kiss me with your tender pouting lips.
punch me in my blushing cheek
just please put some god-damned action into my day-
                  cease it.

introspectioninsightinjusticein -*my-soul* . . . *in-my-life.*
or out of the closets, skeletons haunt
broken bones,
shattered skulls?

drinkyourcoffeesmokethecancerfromyourstick . . .

your cell phone is ringing.

SECOND COMING

i hear the patter of someone's sometimes steps as they walk
away.
almost as a soft rumbling thunder before the skies open
up. God's tears raining
down on the nameless numbers,
as our mist meshes with god's.
the closest i have been to holy in quite some time.
as they say,
"there are no atheists in foxholes.[1]*"*

piece together the drops of water and drink.
drink the nourishment of the tears.
refresh the spirit weak enough to cry.
now god is within.

eruption
fear?,
      angst?,
          content?
              fear? angst?, content?
                     fearangstcontent?

     fear
       angst
         content.

---

[1] William T. Cummings , in C.P. Romulo *I Saw the Fall of the Philippines (1943)*

MOSAIC

every memory blends mundane mosaic
crushed dreams crumble tales we never achieved
regrets dismay clamor together in antic
passion, immoral blend fragrant
                              methane deceived

walk upon faded fantasy
grinding the grains of time
mortal inside
absent cherubic smiles erode
furious paced anarchy lies in life sometimes
innocence fades in a warped nightmare
                              it corrodes

blending clamor coaxed you here
peaceful rest in your grave
your mind wasn't sealed
for your mosaic not complete in your tear
flowing down your cheek for
                              monotony revealed

CIRCUIT

the 5th wheel has fallen off the carriage.
chipped cherry wooden wheels worn by the mileage
      of undervalued,
         maybe overvalued,
            value systems.
planks,
tread,
barbarian,
Michelin,
        babies sit in tires,
               i sit in the tire,
               i rock in the fetal position in hopes
of realizing the circle is not whole.
it is.
it's whole.
when you run full circle,
        its easy to get lost on the cross-section
        of intent
        and predetermination.
determined to run the circuit without thought
to the landmarks which slowly simmer
into the just the broth of memory.
the chicken soup for your flimsy legs
        and more meringue
           mentally
              malleable
               palpable,
                 probable,
                   broken.

4 solid wheels take us around the jaunt,
jived vixens liven the circuitry,
but we all know a circle broken,
     isn't a circle anymore.
the root simmers in the broth of chicken
     and broken wood with
firestone tires bursting
     and toppling suv's.
pre-
de-
term-
i-
nation,
intent
and karma
     swirls
around this circuit,
defective.

like-me-
     and-tonight-
     and-her-
     and-what-i-was-
     and-who-i-am-
     and- where-i-have-gone-
     and-where-i-have-come-from-
     and-where-i-am-going-which-all- seems-to-be-winding-me-
     back-where-i-was-
     and-where-i-belong -
     and -where -i -think -i -was -
     and -where -i -think -i -just -saw -that -landmark -
          but -it -all -looks- the -same -
          but -i -think -i -should -stop -because -i -think- the- other-
               4 -tires -are -' wooden -
     and -wearing- thin -

21

but- i -keep -running -because -i -feel -i -have -to -
but -i -never -stop -because- it- just -seems- appropriate-
not- to-let people- down-
because- i -always -do -
but- i -try -not -to-
because -they-all- depend -on —me ——
but- i -am-weak -
but -there-is- no -time- for -weakness -
and -weakness -only -comes -from -weak- minds -
and -i -am -strong-
because- i -know -where-i -am -go-ing
and -where -i -come- from -
and -where- i -am- now . . .

(breathe)

which ——

is ——————

lost.

COLD WAR (SEEPING)

the cold war ended
        sometime in the 80's.
walls came crumbling down
into heaps of charred asbestos
it was a wonderful thing
brother
        embracing pen,
        embracing brother
new page
same ink
seeps
into the tree.
whose brethren i smoke
and whose distant uncle i recline on.
and we write.
the same recycled ash i flick from the cherry of my cigar
tobacco fumes seep into the freshened ink
led from my pencil seeps into my
        organic daydream
it levitates over my uncle
the creek moseys nowhere
        and the cars overhead speed nowhere.
and the fax will be there before
        two tomorrow
and the trees will be collated
        and stapled before i go to lunch
and the pebbles will be filed before i go home today.
so we can go home organized.
and in a tizzy of confusion

over 3 men asking for a light in Russian
the cold war ended buddy.
its in the memo under the one that says . . .
gone to drowned myself . . .
because i lost sight of myself
on your lunch break
in your office
a few years ago
i think it was the 80's.

BODY TEMPERATURE

ninety-eight point six degrees reflect off the porcelain
                        as relief overwhelms my body
how inopportune a time to think of you.
warmth in the moment and the peaceful sedation
your skin as ivory cool as the porcelain baby-doll.
her painted lucid eyes wind over me.
over ninety-eight point six degrees of warmth.
and cinnamon lips linger in my mind and on my mouth
your ivory cool thumb gently tracing the webs of my fingers
gently zipper my pants and mosey away.
with our inopportune moment inside me
ninety-eight point six degrees safely locked away.

CONFUSED

at first it hurt like a bitch.
but now apathy has entered,
                    invaded,
                    overtaken and
                    destroyed.
you would think that living without a heart would
lessen the pain of other influences
you . . .
            along . . .
                            with . . .
i
would be wrong.

the profuse bleeding from my "heart"
could not be actual blood
for if it was
how would i be able to know i have no love.
love after all does come from the heart
leaving the source of this passiveness rendered . . .
unknown.

my soul must be suspect
after all doesn't your soul give you an identity?
i am just another nameless face
in a world of nameless faces,
                    aren't i?

however my soul is healthy.
heart and soul, yet passiveness reigns the kingdom

27

of . . .
      of . . .
           . . . of
this lack of a meaningless existence.
my will must be suspect to . . .
      to my apathy . . .
but my lack of a will is showing emotion
so maybe apathy isn't what i feel?

      but what is?

SHOOTING STAR (A LIL' FLOW)

wiffle bat smack
lightning bugs fly
fire in the sky
extra terrestrial
e.t. phone home
phone sex operator answers
semen on my playstation
triangle triggers miniskirts

g-spots
p- funk

Clinton got a hummer
mayor smokes a crack pipe
natives smoke a peace pipe
and everything is all
good.
in my village of Mayfair
with no Irish to speak of.
children play Russian roulette
gamblers anonymous has a name
alcoholics anonymous has a name
write it in the sky
with the tails of the lightning bugs
light sabers sear the midnight moon.
good morning '
good night

29

OPHELIA

tears rolling down my face,
drowning in this ocean of agony . . .
when the waves of the tears bombard my soul,
i'm numb from the absence of a will to live . . .

ruptured by the assault of her words,
passion and love severed with a knife . . .
all i did was let passion burn in my soul,
now the breeze of silence smothers the flair . . .

Good night, ladies, good night, sweet ladies, good night, good night. [2]

---

[2] Final words of Ophelia in Shakespeare's masterpiece Hamlet.

JOURNEY

do i have the durability
to walk through hell alone?
for i sleep upon these fires,
i sleep all alone.

i sleep upon these nails,
constantly driving into my flesh.
i arise each day with a new scar upon my soul.
i arise each day with a new scar upon my flesh.

isolated, i spend my life.
i face life's obstructions secluded.
i walk through, through persisting lonesome.
      i walk.
      i walk alone.

33

-SIMM

ANOTHER DAY ON SEPTA³

southbound scramble frantic   *watch the closing doors.*
toss my worn body sloppily into the
  not so quiet
  not quite "bucket" seats.
sighhhhhhhhhhhh
my head goes down to ponder the day when it
  all————————————————
  slows————————————————
  down————————————————

our eyes never locked,
our voices never tickle-me-elmo-ed each others eardrums.
  what did happen?
  what did happen?

i didn't mean to stare,
although i know i probably did.
i was engaged to be married,
without knowing your name,
or hearing your voice.

you smiled at a baby. and
i could only stare at you. i
am sure the baby was cute though. i
was staring at you. and your
dimple, on your left cheek accentuated
perfectly by the perfectly placed freckle.

i think my mother will love you.
she has a thing for a woman with a fashion sense and
a perfectly placed freckle especially one
that accentuates a dimple. could
you wave at me and not the baby?
don't get up!
where is my solace,
come back.

southbound
scramble-frantic   *watch the doors please*

---

[3] Septa- South Eastern Pennsylvania Transportation Authority. Bus system in Phila-
delphia.

TODAY

hidden under superficial scars,
protecting lust aged with neglect.
when venial blood starts dripping from my flesh,
vibrant smiles start gracing my wounds.

kidnap innocence of youth,
feeding rabid hunger for genocide
with the key to my soul un
      locked
peer into the au-
          then
          ticity of rage.
savage passion
      for what
no one can grasp.
intangible lusts
      misunderstood
      for what
question my existence?
how can you question
      insanity?

Rest in peace, those who have passed too soon. Especially those who
have touched my life. Also those who died in the terrorist attack on 9/11/
01. God Bless everyone who lost someone in this senseless attack

37

SJMM

SOCIOPATH

you can't see me
        (because i am inside you.)
not part of you,
        (but controlling you.)
ball of clay molded into my phallic tool to probe
probe inside of you., can you feel my presence
i pinch your nerves c5 to c6[4]
broken spine
you can't move
        (without me.)
i am your wheelchair
wheeled down i95[5]
at 5 miles per hour
as the Camay's cruise past at 75.
the fast lane of broken aides
        (because i can break you.)
        (because i am you.)
i cut small holes
in your leaky valves
        (and bleed you . . .)
from the inside out.
you call me a sociopath
        (but you created me)
you played the deist
        (and i denied your prayers)
the phone line is busy
i am out to lunch
i eat a piece of flesh
and smoke a Marlboro

39

as i remember skull-fucking you
and as i sit here
i wonder what it would be like
to involve your wife
            (and her pretty red lace panties)
she seems to be intrigued
as we eat
            (and she tells me how naughty
            she has been
            and plans to be)
are you uneasy friend
you should be, she is so tender to my touch

---

[4] Discs in the human back.

[5] Highway along the east coast of the US.

IMBALANCE

you want to talk about chemical imbalances.
you can't balance your judgements
    or scales on
    dizzy spells
    and fallen golden cows[6].
i have become an addict.
i know it
i admit it
along the way, the shepherd lost me
wandering on the superfund site[7] scale of your plateaued land
unsupervised, i stepped into the acid and morphed into what
                you want to pity.
was i lost at three, maybe four
GI Joe marched into the linguistics laboratory
and now you want a thread to weave a storyline
a storyline into a basket to hold the fruit of my labor
miscarriage
voices dwindle down into my own.
GI Joe
        and the shepherds
               and the teachers
                     and the network of clusterfuck
of the once
        past
           present
               future bickering of jumbled jargon

snow on the television
channel ninety nine shows a shepherd stranded in melting

> he's melting,
> he's melting,
> he's melting

---

[6] Old Testament reference. Moses came down the mountain from talking to God, to see that his people were worshiping a Golden Calf.

[7] Toxic waste dumps, being cleaned by environmentalists.

HEROIN

ignite my veins with the wrath of your impassioned
                                        soothing
                                        lullaby.
rock me to sleep with the pitch of your voice.
it slithers through the night.
cold sweets,
        humid,
        damp,
        moist,
mommy change me.
hold me, i had a nightmare.
i can't wake from this scary dream.
scary reality?
(is it reality?)
mommy, i can't feel your touch.
(are you touching me?)
i can feel the goosebumps on my neck,
(is that the caress of evil?)
mommy, i'm scared.
broken chariots pull the day from the night.
unveil the virgin in her beauty.
mommy
i'm scared.
mommy?

CHILDISH LOVE

hide and seek, hearts only suffer.
solitude singular alone.
quake in the caress of my down quilt.
remember what was..
what is?
this is what's left? the game?
the shoots and ladders of memories slipping and ascending
                                    more slipping than ascending.
slipping slipping slipped into
                        the solitude singular alone state.
the state of candyland.
the sugar sweets rot my teeth that chew your trust.
indigestion,
heartburn
Rolaids?

45

THE FLAVOR OF SELF MEDICATION

kill the patient
if you can't find the problem
don't infect yourself
with carcinogen flavored popcorn
processed cheese sprinkled radon daughters tasty,
      lingering
in the iv bag.
          drip
          drip
          drip
faucets clink as i urinate all over the wall
pink floyd escapes my radio
transistors quack, my nose bleeds
powder sugah so sweet from the convience store
i'm not missing, neither is the flavor.
Wisconsin's finest dairy machines pop out some prosaic
      like the pill,
      like the time released gelatin flavor
your only sick if you have the symptom
nothing bothers me
rotten from the inside out
you never feel what
you cannot process.

BLACK COFFEE

the first sip of steaming coffee is always so bitter.

                               in the morning

maybe its me.

maybe i don't stir the sugar enough.

the sugar settles in the bottom of the cup and melts

                      while i wince from the bitterness.

how can people take coffee black?

how can i comprehend what it means to drink black coffee.

i need to be sweetened.

                  and creamed

                      and taken to the dance

before dropping my dollar, so

i tolerate that first bitter sip.

because i know the last sip will be a double shot

of sweet chUrry pie.

so i drink from my styrofoam friend.

          in my middle class

               socioeconomic comfortable world.

asking why drink black coffee?

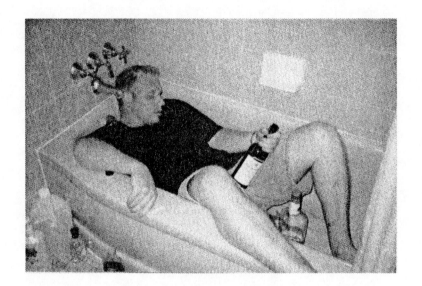

I COULDN'T BEHOLD MY LOVER

i couldn't behold my lover
for honesty
       had driven us apart.
jealousy's diffusion,
i lost all rationale.
i scoured below the cold pits of the earth.
i couldn't behold my lover, i found you.
    her~
    cold~
    taste ,
the coldness reminded me of you.
she trickled down my throat.
    moist
    tender
    poppy craven cured
hours upon hours,
i lie in apathy.
with her remains by my side.
yearning for you,
    she pleased me.
i despised myself for my pleasure
    i couldn't behold my lover.
    i couldn't behold your love.
    i couldn't behold my anger.
      i had to submit
        to her.
yearning for you, i lie beside her in apathy.
disgusted by my own presence

49

i still yearn for you.
jealousy is spreading
i lie in apathy.

ILLUSIONS OF LIGHT

you can say forever
i only say for what
together 2 candles burn into one
i still can't own the idea of light
the blackened bird only sees through blackened eyes.
i am a crow
shrieking on the perched wire
absorbed in thought no one could decode
you hear a cry
but you see no tears
drenched rags held close to my chest
hold my wings tight
you only see black
matching my aura
if you look hard enough at black,
        you might see purple
                insecure, scared
look harder
        you might see shades of blue.
                    Atlas[8], oh, the pressures of being godly.

---

[8] Greek titan who was cursed to hold the sky on his shoulders for eternity.

HEAVENLY

i'd be an alcoholic,
    if i could afford it.
i'd swim in vodka and
    taste every shot of sherry
i'd appreciate the illness for what its worth.
its an escape from section 9 housing,
        kids r us kids
        and politicians.

Pontius Pilate[9] briefly washed his hands
of conscience before his damnation of guilt.
is Pontius in heaven?
can pilot drink the wine from the chalice of the lord?
can he drink of the blood of christ, even
if he is the one who spilled it?

excuse me, can i wash my hands?
i have some contemplation to consider
i turn the wet rusty handle of the sink to realize the wetness, isn't water,
its blood.
the blood of christ dripping from the nails that pierced his wrists.
maybe i should call my buddy Pilate.
we have some reflecting to do,
        and the game is on in 5 minutes anyway.

---

[9] Judge who gave orders to crucify Jesus. According to scripture, he washed his
hands for a long time before ruling on Jesus' fate.

21

children giggle with glee
    in their tummies.
walking by the games i once lost.
my path leads me not
    to the playground.
    the corner bar
fields my stimulation.
    i haven't grown up.
    i have grown cynical.
look at those games,
i know i have gotten older.
    but have i grown?
has the seasoning of years
marinated a man in juices of jaded memories?
bury my soul in liquid comfort.
toss back trinkets of lost time.
hit the back of my pallet, hit the back of my brain.
    21 years,
    21 horse pills to swallow whole.
no apple sauce to coat the flavor.
can't break down the medication to stop my gag reflex
the savory flavor makes me gag.
    my tummy aches.

-SIMM

GRACE

gentle grace in a stride of radiance.
with tails of emotion yielding waves of attraction
eyes closed with the openness of the want
eyes open with the feelings of the need
eyes open with the feelings of desire
the lone desire to hold you close
the itch in my eyes
in hopes of someday,
holding the radiance in your tails
to experience the gentle grace.

SIMM

DEAREST JAMIE, (A LOST GENERATION)

i'm not sleeping well.
maybe it's the humidity
or maybe it's what's been on my mind for the past year.
maybe it's the fact you always want what you can't have or
maybe, it's just the humidity.

i have a million and one thoughts running
through my head.
i built a barrier up to hold back all the bullshit
i felt because,
i wanted to hate you.
i do hate you.
fuck
what i said earlier.
that's politically correct me, and
i don't feel much like being PC right now,
so fuck that.
fuck it all.

i don't get hurt anymore.
i am a machine.
i haven't felt since some trick back in the day
who played her games with me.
i give people just enough me to make them think they know me,
and
i smile on the inside because they only know what
i want them to know.
i am a machine.
i don't feel.

i let you feel what i want you to feel and,
i move on with my day.
its the way computers work.
your either alive or dead, and
    i am without question dead.
    i like it that way.
        you can't get hurt, even with barriers built.

so i took the train home with you.
    i felt like a fucking school girl.
    i laughed and i totally forgot my terminator[10]/
        Arnold[11]/
        rebel without a cause[12]
        attitude.
    i was too caught up in you.
    i never got a chance to build my barrier with you.
    i hate you for that.
    i hate you for making me be as naked as a neonatal crack baby
        and just as weak.

    i can't blame you for what you did.
in life, you have to look out for number one.
    i always did.
except with that trick-ass-bitch
        and you.
people speculate what's wrong with the world,
what's wrong with our *generation*,
    i have the answer.

---

[10] 1984 movie Starring Arnold Schwarzenegger.

[11] Arnold Schwarzenegger- action movie star/ body builder.

[12] 1955 movie starring James Dean.

-SIMM

don't tell anyone though.
the answer is we think with our heads way to fucking much.
we like computers

                                        and cars
                                    and TV shows.

these things are all mechanical.
they all have ways to be fixed.
that's something humans don't have.
there isn't always a way to be fixed.

sometimes things break.
            i have a parent that i teach his daughter.
                        he is 30 years old.
                    he has a newborn baby.
            he is one of the best people i have ever met.
                    he lost his job last week.
        he found out he has inoperable cancer. this week
                    he is a walking dead man.
                    he is broken and
                    he can't be fixed.

            i am broken, because
            i made a mistake.
            i made a mistake just like you did on a few occasions.
you told me there was a chance.
whenever it was,
                        you told me you could love me.
            i made the mistake of believing you.
            i was wrong for not building that barrier.
            i chose not to think with my head.
you asked me why i cared about you.
            i opened my heart.
                                        again, no barrier.

i got burned.
you slept with 5 guys in one night,
        i opened my heart,
and forgave you.

                                    again, no barrier.

maybe that last one wasn't you
                            but you get the idea.
its broken not because you were selfish.
                                but because i was weak.
        i was weak for believing in smiles in a cheesy El train.
for some weird feeling i get in the pit of my stomach
                                that caused me to trust.
that is not your fault.
so for that fact,
        i am sorry.
        i placed undue pressure on your shoulders.
        i'm broken,
        not you.

you can't blame me though.
the only regrets in life are the chances you never take.
i laid it out there because i felt stronger than i ever had before.
        i saw you hurting, and
        i would have walked on broken glass to make you feel joy for a
    momentary second.
        i knew you were dying and
        i point blank lied to you tonight.
        i said
        i didn't know you were vulnerable.
        i fucking knew.
        i was just too weak of a man to admit that
        i needed you to see me, instead of some cat who didn't realize
    what he lost.

                              he is lost,
                              he thought with his head.
                              he's from our generation.
          the lost *generation.*

so i am asking myself . . .
                                        was it worth it in the end.
          i will never admit that i cried because i am working on building
barriers.
          i did go through the most intense typing that
          i ever managed to finger when
          i told you how
          i felt.
          i lost a dream, a fantasy and a soul mate.
          i gained the knowledge that
                                        my *generation* is lost.
          i gained the sleepless night of humidity typing on blind eyes.
but
          i lost you. and
          i gained feeding your ego. and
          i lost my pride.

you probably can't
                                        comprehend this,
or choose not to
                                        comprehend this, and
          i don't blame you.
your probably using your head,
                                        and that's not your fault,
                                           its our generation.

so as
          i said tonight.
          i have been engaged.
          i have been in love.

60

but the most intensity
    i have felt to date is with you on the El with cheesy smiles.
take it for what it's worth,
               but take it wherever you go.
because for all the pain and barriers knocked down on that el.
    i always have those memories of you.
no matter how weak
    i am, or you think
    i am,
    i know what was there.
(deep inside
    i still know you do too. but
    i'm not going there because
    i have to start thinking with my head.)

thank you for reading, good-bye
me

p.s.- yes,
    i still hate you.

-SIMM

MARTYR

you hang on a crucifix.
bound by fisherman's knots.
fishing for telecomunicatory compliments
your frail neck slides to the left.
situate your grimy hair that
                slid into your gelatin green eyes
you pout your lips
you want sympathy
i give it
your pain suspends
mine initiates

the ties *(the lies) (the eyes)* unwind as the splinters of the rope become
                verbal lashes *(eyelashes)* across my salty back
i look into your unmerciful sage
                i ask for more.
your emotional masochistic sadism, i wear leather.
warm un-breathing flesh hugs my genitals too close.
your boot thrust into my abdomen.
as your hair flows in the breeze of electric fans.
                your scarf flows, delicate
your wince rounds into pleasurable smiles
until i grab your throat and pounce
your carcass to the cross where you belong . . .
breathless trout
                pout
                        and perish.

IDENTIFY ME

identify me as urban
raised with the roaches
    live or smoked
short me a cigarette
2 bucks a pack
a nicfit from snapping
she snapped her body suit [13]
and her body was traced.
i unsnapped her body suit
and her body was laid
A dancer on my stage
it was a shame we were
only 13

identify me as urban
inner city punk
    punk or be punked
dealing by the streetlight
daylight savings
    like anyone can tell the difference
can you tell the difference
am i just uneducated
in the dark or under your brightness
doubt it, pop

identify me as urban
a pest in your view
the roaches dealing by the streetlights
uneducated punks

finding ways sink
shame i popped that body suit
she was so fragile
she wasn't scared
shame i popped that body suit
she called me daddy
although she was your seed
don't worry
she didn't bleed
much.

---

[13] Suit worn traditionally by dancers. They are form fitting, one-piece, that usually
are fastened at the crotch

-SIMM

NURTURE

stop hearing and listen to the context clues curated by my clever mouth.
muscles moving abusing the cannon.
mold me in uncomfortable wooden chairs
so i can
listen

stop looking and see the symmetry of today and yesterday
nothing new, something old retold, repackaged, reviled
mold me in uncomfortable wooden chairs
so i can
learn.

stop eating and taste the morsels of malicious malice.
taste the moment, and spit it if the flavor doesn't suffice.
mold me in uncomfortable wooden chairs
so i can
hunger.

stop snorting and smell the fragrances of futile fucking quick-fixes.
smell the aroma of misled mothers and fucked up fathers.
mold me in uncomfortable wooden chairs
so i can
learn

mold me in uncomfortable wooden chairs
so i can
listen

mold me in uncomfortable wooden chairs
so i can
hunger

mold me in uncomfortable wooden chairs
so i can
revolt

SIMM

BUS RIDE

intent.
intend.
intense
intertwine.
fall apart.
lost in a road of regret and unlived dreams.
children sleep on the mother's lap.
her preoccupation with the newspaper suppresses maternal love.
stroke the baby's hair.
such a precious love, absent.
headlines always over instincts.
sounds shriek.
gunshots sizzle and destroy as baby suddenly wakes.
headlines over instinct.
drink the lifeblood of this society.
warm the innards of middle class america, malcontent.
headlines mesmerize and coffee slithers over the seat.
a liquid ball room dance across the mercury floor.
chocolate warm elegance.
less warm, more awkward fat man plops down.
no more dancing.
baby cries.
intense
intend
intertwine
fall
            apart.

69

INHALE

i thought of a brilliant poem
         in my mind
but i didn't have a pen to ink it.
i know i swallowed a bumblebee
         and it bolistically flickered in my chest,
stars dimming, dots of knowledge
                  and understanding
                           and love

levitating consonants
                  and vowels
i try to catch
                  i gently paw at the air's feline sheepishness
Mary lands on my fingers
                  i take her to my mouth
                           and kiss her so pillow softly
the butterflies
                  swirl in my pooh belly
                           and in my lungs
it was nice. . . .

BIRTH

i give birth with my legs closed
silver awnings shelter my privacy
      intimacy
in the lightning storm, my acid rain reflux can only be
controlled by pepcid
i give you life
carbon,
   i mean silicon,
   i mean neutrons, protons, electrons
   and beyond
don't you dare tell me i'm alone
because i have you
and you are with me in my shelter
homeless street civilians refuse to have help.
pride is in the sewage steam grates they sleep on.
press off my armani suit sweetheart.
press conferences, my baby is born in Portland,
   i mean Philly
   i mean piss off
i have too much pride too pussy.

VIRGINITY

caress my neck.
is everything going to be ok?
reassure me
                you still need me.
wander through my eyes.
as i glide my fingers through~your~cornsilk.
beauty is
only skin deep,
can souls mesh for eternity?
tickle my back as i hold your hips.
tell me your fears . . .
                and your dreams . . .
                and your hopes . . .
is it ok to be scared?
how long is eternity?
do you care either?

TRIP

teddy bear porn
and roses made of concrete
fairy dust from sandman
brimming with caffeine
children with their tongues
wagging
acid dropped
cottonmouth candycorn
cotton plants have thorns
                              too
too much stone pricking my finger
a cotton picking shame
the cotton candy corn in my cottonmouth
treats for me
lollipops and gummybears
bears hugging too close for the cubs to see
cottonmouth candycorn and pricking thorns
                          to boot.

SHUT UP

do you know your melancholy banter is trivial at best?
melodramatic mind numbing reruns of old 90210's.[14]
incoherent babble pollutes the
                                    air
                                    you know.
someone call the fucking EPA[15].
droop your puppy-dog eyes
              and tell
              me again,
oops,
i heard that one yesterday,
and you probably plan on telling me tomorrow
              don't cha?
ramble, ramble, ramble,
do you now feel pacified?
i hope you feel guilty:
you made me write this horrible poetry.
it's a shame though,
i want to love you.
i already lust for you.
i just wish i could
              tolerate you.

---

[14] Aaron Spelling television show geared towrds a female demographic. First aired
October 4, 1990
[15] Enviornmental Protection Agency.

THE CIRCUS

its all in front of me.
as everything i thought
        . . . i thought
was left behind.
with too much emotional baggage to carry on my own heart strings.
even with a valet with as much makeup as you.

we can't hold it.
these decisions have the stability of a fucking tightrope.
i don't remember being trained as an acrobat . . .
        is there a net to catch me?
are the clowns up to there old games
cutting down the strings that hold my fate?
this circus doesn't have a ringmaster.
no one can put order into this anarchy stricken sovereignty
that is myself, yourself and
        themselves . . .
uncertain dreams ready to poof at any second..
        or have they disintegrated from the monotony that seems
        to override the
        anarchy
monotonous anarchy?
yeah . . .
    right . . .
        sure . . .
           pal . . .

welcome home...?

MISLED

spoon
fed
know
ledge
yield
ing
ethics
taint~
ed
with lies . . .
with mis
guided
thoughts
down your
yellow brick road.
i got lost
on the way
home.

-SIMM

AFTER SEEING DESIREE

smooth as a San Franciscan earth rattling quake.
uproot the basis of the conscious mind.
logic?
what is logic, when you stand in front of me?
foundations of fundamental humanities support
indecisive definitive positions,
                    decisions and
                    eventual debacles.
abuse the Pavlovian laws[16],
theorize my debonair expressions.
riding along on my white horse,
a knight of your fancy.
what happens when i drop you?
quakes uproot the unconscious mind?
quakes uproot the conscious mind.

---

[16] Theory of classical conditioning. Conditioned responses are strengthened with repetition under renforcement

MANUFACTURED

build me up,
        to tear me down
wallpaper me in confederate money[17]
to remind me of my forefathers fuck up
show me the past
        so i can live in it
        and analyze it
like Freud and his crack addiction
i run from it
        to find it
repackage it
in a new professional wrestling gimmick

there is a picture of you in my wallet
i take it out from time to time
wallets hold identity,
        you know the gimmick abuse
        and some repackaged condoms
Fort Sumter[18] revisited
Sherman[19] lighting your pic on fire
you would think the burn would sting
it doesn't
it resonates
        in it's crispy past

---

[17] Money distributed by southern states during American Civil War.

[18] Place of the opening battle of the American Civil War.

[19] Northern General who burned down 140 miles of southern lands during American Civil War.

ON YOUR LEVEL

speak from the silt.
reason with the mind impure.
journeys complete through ivory curtains.
curtains curtailing the fucked concepts.
        take me by the hand into the silt.
        cover my venison in your bog.
i clench the soil in my fragile hands,
and encode my venison with your feces.
i massage the debris into my eyes.
i try to attain the visions you considered.
i see shit.

lay in the bathtub of your rinse.
        submerge in your scum.
        open my mouth to drink your verbiage.
all i taste is piss.
        speak to me from the silt.
reason with the mind impure.

-SIMM

CHURCH

the day was new.
the sun danced in my shadow
tickled my steps
with the graceful silk slippers
gliding across my cool solid floor.
they marveled
the cherubs that did the ballet
on my floor. they respected
more than that, they loved.

chivalry died
   but respect forgot to show at the funeral.
lady love and sir dignity were engaged to wed,
   until sweaty lust met meager stupidity and crashed the
   wedding.
innocence was to be christened this morning,
   until she spread her legs for the passional thrust and a fleeting
   breath.

no more silky slippers gliding with the giggling voices in my halls.
no more dancing,
no more sun raising,
no more hope.————————

         no need.

IDLE HANDS

idle hands do the devils work
the devil has blue jeans and no cause
rebel without a whim
> or a dream
> or shoes to take him there

where?
why care?
why are you interested in the devil?
> sinful eyes
>> against christ
>> against gap
> against the democratic republic of my ass

the boil of society
the waste of your misconstrued hands
Mozart conducts a symphony in power chords
with hookers turning a trick
Mozart is a pimp
devil in blue jeans with no cause and a rolex watch
ticking
> ticking
>> ticking

timberland boots with no soul,
> no tapping rhythm
> no traction

ticking
> ticking
>> ticking

power cords
       blue jeans
              what cause
what rebel?
       just power chords
                 and idle hands

SOLID

delicate strokes from stained green eyes
indicate she could be the one
her easy curved smile
and gentle blink melt my defenses
and make my emotions tremble,
                    (knees knock.)
knock on the door
"hello" says the heart as its energy
sends warm sensations sizzling through my stomach
i look in your direction
                    all i see is you
i look away
                    and all i remember is you
i close my eyes
                    and all i sense is you
                    and yearn to sense more of you
                    and smell you
i am a melted man
i sizzle
i evaporate
into the air
hoping to be breathed in by you
so i can be inside you
the warmest place in the world
is inside a woman
and inside you,
i could be solid again

HEAD GAMES

ig
nor
ance
is
your
art~form
with your
master-
piece
paint~ed
with my
face
with my
blood
crimson,
red ab-
stract
all i
see is
the rage
in your
eyes

in your
fucked up
play
you cast
me as
the prince

a puppet
in your
hands
you pull
my veins
see my
re-
act
ions
you see————————————————
you laugh.

FOOD POISONING

should i apologize for my words being so harsh?
should i be sympathetic for my transcribed
 misinterpreted ingenious
 being mistaken for immature ignorance.
is my ignorance a distraction from what you want the
 impressionable to engrave?
sketch your bullshit on my grave and call it artwork.
call all the tragedy that is you,
 i
 and them
 . . . artwork.
place a little apple sticker in the upper left hand corner
and hang it on your infernal refrigerator.
keep your veggies cold
 but your heart colder.
toss a salad fresh with sacred hearts, untainted eyes, and tender lips.
dressing could be the ever sour tears from the prodded eyes.
callous . . .
callous could be the diagnosis.
your queasy stomach must be from the salad.

EVERY MORNING

i can't wake up without a blast of caffeine every morning
exploding magmatic blaze sears
        the fleshy muscle in my filmy mouth.
a wake up call from my middle of the road maid.
she raises my mold~less manhood.
some mornings it just comes to me.
and others it escapes like a wounding breath.
after being kicked in the chest
pounding bradykinin[20],
that's it, i need some brandy in this coffee.
swallow the bruise in my belly.
just to wake up,
on this freaking
        thursday
           morning.

---

[20] Chemical that causes discoloration in human bruises.

SIMM

TEENAGER

i opened my eyes this morning
     and came to the stiff realization
     that i was repulsive
the mirror's language laughed at the image
as i ran cold water over my bitter beaten face
the wet ice dripping down my frozen frown
traced my robust nose.
thin chapped lips and puss filled pores
i woke up and acquired the perception of what the world
must have seen so long ago.
they see the laughter of the mirror
they see the frown for what it is
they see it as a mask to hide my hypersensitive feelings
just beginning to be embraced by someone
          anyone
isn't that all we need?
someone to rub the nape of our
neck when the stones pile up
that builds a dam holding back the wet frozen ice.
      or the molten rocks
      or the empty wetness
from my sockets
and it all traces back to that mirror.
and that damn realization
damn i am repulsive
and now bloody
fuck that mirror
and fuck you for looking.

-SIMM

CLOSE YOUR EYES

in
the early
morning
if
you
can wake up
that early
there
is a
time
when the
world
is
tranquil
yes,
even
in the city.
when
the cars
nap
and the
crickets
cease.
there
is no
sun
no
moon
and if

you
pretend
hard enough
not
even
a
you

A.C.

man has intrinsic needs
instinctual survival dependencies
like this neon[23],
        crying as we punch 90 down the expressway.

2 dollars
        a need
gas money
        a need
85 cent tolls
        a need
speed, adrenaline
i need insulin
the needs of a diabetic
un-sugar-coated bliss, rolling to A.C.[24]

the air drills rigidly through my locks
breathe in the decayed fish and the cotton candy giggles
the wind howls
        like you did
i grow to love the air,
        like i grew to love you
i accept the carbonated cork popping needs
i still have trouble accepting you
so i roll up my window.

---

[23] Type of car.

[24] Atlantic City, New Jersey.

-SIMM

the air still creeps with the charm of a hurricane
the other window won't let me forget.
my cheek slapped around,
        wind burn,
        red. . . . flush
        flush the toilet
        flush the vagina

i fear the air because
i need the air
i once needed something more
some say it was love
      i say it's misplaced cell phone calls
        on the a.c. expressway[25]
      lost signals on overpriced cell phones
but don't look back on the a.c. expressway at four
      in the morning
all you see is black.

---

[25] Highway connecting parts of New Jersey to the southern Jersey beaches.

COLD WAR II

i started to type this poem in rage filled italics.
             in bold face.
then i realized the ramifications of keyboard strokes
or worse
the lack of my loyal quill
separation anxiety, panic attacks in Siberia.
snow boarders cut 360 olleys in church pews
             at St. Petersburg cathedral.
need more prayers?
i need the sense to know the splicing of keyboard poetry.
irritate ivory strokes in the bathroom confessional.
the KGB[21] stands over me as i shiver,
naked in the eye of the snowstorm.
watched by snowboarders in fancy red hats and
             fluffy warm coats.
with my keyboard cord around my neck.
double clicked mouse
mice crawling under my skin
bubonic[22] plagued feces
dsl, 56k, Cuban missiles
suicide on the information superhighway.

---

[21] Secret police/intelligence agency of the Soviet Union.

[22] A.k.a. Black Death. Disease that wiped out large numbers beginning in the 14th century. Later used as biological warfare.

HEY BRIAN

i'm not going to your funeral.
       call it selfish,
       call it immature
       call it self preservation.
a man to man defense
       in a zoned out kinda world.
i chose not to play the games .
you were always on the edge,
       i was always jumping over it.
somehow, you slipped into the coffin and
       i jumped, here.

the bathroom of the 210 hallway, dingy
               smelled like donkey piss,
yet the legacy squirts through the dingy syringes.
from before our reign until way after our demise.
i was there for the heat,
       the suck,
       the boot,
       and the blast.
fuck, we went to algebra class right after.
       trinomials,
       try this shit,
       try to recognize the flavor of a fifty bag.
even an algebraic equation can see
that smack plus disenchanted youth equals two candidates for rehab
       . . . or one dead and one fatally wounded spirit.

i got out when it got
     too real, too fake.
like the tears at your funeral will likely bring.
men in cheap black suits and cheap black ties,
saying "why, i don't understand."
they never do,
remember when we were
     too good for that shit.
we played the speed game.
man to man in algebra was never
     so much fun.
algebra was never
     so real
     so fake.
clammy skin was never
     so real, so fake.
swish, just gimme the rock baby,
     i'm on fire.

how long ago was 4th grade?
defibrillation,
     not incantation
          not death
              and certainly not us.
i teach kids now,
i wanted to go back and see where we got lost.
     maybe backtrack,
     maybe become a man.
i sure don't feel like one christening this piece with my tears.
     too real, too fake.

-SIMM

i'm not going to the funeral.
i'm not looking in the casket and regretting.
    i know it could have been me in there just like
    i know it could have been me striking out to end the season that
year.
    i know it could have been me who humped your girlfriend.
    i know it could have been me who shot up way too much, way
                 too often with way
                 too lost of a stare,
    i know it could have been me in the rehab, or me falling back
    into the need.
one day at a time is
    too real too fake.
sitting with these kids is
    too real too fake.
22 years of losing yourself in an algebraic chemical equation with
unbalanced corrosive variables is
    too real too fake.
why can't we just admit we were
    too real too fake.
the 210 hallway and dirty needles were
    too real too fake.
now you are
    too dead
    too real,
    too fake
and i am
    too alive
    to fall back in-
    to the scene
    too much
    too little
    to gamble anymore.

i'm sorry i can't take it in the foot with you one more time.
or watch you bust your ass on your skateboard,
or bust the teachers balls in class.
it's been

> *too long and i'm*
> *too selfish*
> *too go*
> back
> *to the*
> *too real*
> *too fake life.*

it's been four years since i've seen you and
four years

> *to forget that world.*

we are just a notch on the 210 hallway's post.

> *too real,*
> *too fake*
> *to pinch veins and*

say goodbye when i've already did it my own way

> *so long ago.*

sincerely,
Shawn

BACKWARDS (ACKNOWLEDGEMENTS)

In case I never get to do this again, I want to thank those who have helped in this process.

Dad, Thanks for being there every step of the way. Kerry, thanks for being a brother and growing to be a friend. Heather, keep him in line! Uncle Rob, the coolest old guy I know. Midgie, where are my jelly cookies? Marie Smolenski, my 2nd mom, thanks for the camera and your support! And everyone else who shares the bloodlines with me, here's to you. Jim, Kathy, and Tom O thanks for being friends.

My friends who have helped with the book
Nick Smolenski- Artwork

> Nick, I wish I could put into words how much it meant to work with you on this project. You truly are an artistic genius, a musical prodigy and above all that, a friend. Odd Man Out, Disorder and h8 LIVE!

Innersha- Contributing artist

> Teenager pic's artist. One of the most talented artists I have ever had the privilege of knowing. Watch out for him, he is going to be big.

Sean Berk- editor

> Sean, You truly are the one that convinced me that I could chase this dream. I always knew I wanted it, but you sold me on the idea for that, I am eternally grateful. Through the performances, beer pong tournaments, and whining kids, I found a true friend.

Christine Ridgley- editor

> To think, we wasted all that energy hating each other. Thanks for ripping apart my grammar and punctuation, you're going to be an amazing English teacher. You're still a bitch and a pool nazi.

109

Steven Watson- Web master

Steve, You are an amazing stranger who has reinstalled my faith in humanity. I didn't know you from Adam when we met, but you helped me when I needed it most. Thanks for all your time and effort in this process!

All the models who put up with Nick and I, Thank You

Jamie Stires, "Soccer Mom" Bridgette Bond, Suzanne O'Donnell, Christa Sauer, Colleen Kelly, Mike Smolenski, Christine Ridgley, Sandy "The greatest waitress ever" and Chuck Sherwood.

Special Thanks to the following-

Phil Stevens- thanks for pointing me in the right direction. Angela Gaio- My best friend without ever seeing you. Thanks for your silent and vocal support. Jennifer Miller- has been reading my crap since I started. Christine Adams- My first love and inspiration to start writing. Michelle A Smith- Thanks for letting me speak to your classes and pollute their minds.

Teachers shape minds, thanks for molding me. Colleen Clark, Carol Lechlikner, Dolores Hughes, Jefferson Slatoff, Ms. Soifer, Phil Stevens.

Naked eyes,
      naked heart,
            bare shadows
                  baring blush.
LEAVE purity.
      Learn from my purity.
            A purity that knows no question is trivial,
and no observation comes without more questioning.

Want more?

Visit Simmons' web site…

Http://question-of-reality.tripod.com

Info on
future release dates
performances
direct contact with the poet and artist

Printed in the United States
4830